Monitoring Your Child's iMessages and Text Messages

A Step by Step Guide

Ted Mitchell

www.ianswerguy.com

Table of Contents

Preface

Parents face a difficult challenge in this high-tech age. There are more ways than ever for kids to communicate. Concerned parents want to stay involved and understand what their kids are doing, but often it is difficult to keep pace with all the technology. This guide is intended to help parents cut through some of the technology and use it to monitor their child's iPhone messages.

This guide is written for Apple devices such as the iPhone, iPad, and iPod touch that use iMessage. It is not intended for non-Apple devices.

You will need to know your child's Apple ID and password to use the techniques described in this guide. Additionally, the device you use to monitor your child's messages will need to be connected to the Internet at all times, either with a Wi-Fi network or a cellular data network.

If you have a question at any point while reading this, please don't hesitate to contact me on my website www.ianswerguy.com. I would also appreciate any feedback you would like to share.

1   Understanding iPhone Messages

The Messages app on the iPhone is capable of sending and receiving SMS text messages, MMS messages, and iMessages. To monitor your child's messages, it helps to understand a little about these various types of messages.

SMS Text Messages

SMS stands for Short Message Service. SMS text messages are the basic text messages that have been used for years, even before smartphones ever existed.

When you send a message from your iPhone to someone with a basic cell phone (non-smartphone) or any smartphone other than an iPhone (Android, BlackBerry, Windows…), your iPhone will automatically send the message as an SMS text.

When an SMS text message is sent on the iPhone, the message is displayed with a green background.

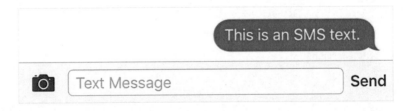

Your cellular provider manages the delivery of an SMS text message to the recipient's phone number. Regular texting rates will apply, based on your texting plan from your cellular provider.

MMS Messages

MMS stands for Multimedia Messaging Service. MMS messages are similar to SMS text messages except they contain a multimedia file, such as a photo. When you create a text message and attach a photo, you are sending an MMS message.

MMS messages require an active cellular data network to send the message. Most cellular providers do not count an MMS message against your monthly data limit. However, contact your cellular provider if you have any questions about how MMS messages are handled on your cellular plan.

iMessages

The iMessage service from Apple is an alternative to the SMS and MMS messages from your cellular provider. The iMessage service allows messages to be sent between Apple devices such as the iPhone, iPad, iPod touch, and Mac computers. This is convenient because an iMessage can be sent or received on devices that would not normally be able to send an SMS or MMS message, such as the iPad, iPod touch, and Mac computer.

When an iMessage is sent, the message is displayed with a blue background.

An iMessage can only be sent between Apple devices.

The iMessage service can be used on an iPhone, iPad, iPod touch, or a Mac computer. This versatility is due to iMessage being related to your Apple ID. Any device that is setup to use your Apple ID is capable of sending or receiving iMessages. If you have an iPhone, the phone number is also associated with your Apple ID and all devices using your Apple ID can receive iMessages sent to your phone number.

In the upcoming sections, we will explore how to use the versatility of iMessage to monitor your child's messages.

Other Types of Messages

There are a wide variety of free messaging apps available in the App Store. Some examples of the messaging apps are TextFree, Text+, TextMe, and TextNow.

Your child can also use apps such as WhatsApp, Viber, Snapchat, Instagram, and Facebook Messenger to communicate with their friends. The list of messaging options is almost endless.

While iMessages and SMS text messages are frequently used, it is important to understand other messaging options are also available.

This guide is intended to show you how to monitor your child's iMessages and potentially his/her SMS and MMS messages. Messages from other apps cannot be monitored using the techniques discussed in this guide. If you want to monitor messages from these other apps, your options are much more limited. At the end of this guide, we will discuss some possible monitoring options using professional monitoring services or monitoring software for your computer.

2 Overview

In this section we will explore how the versatility of iMessage can be used to monitor your child's messages.

Before we get started with iMessage, it helps to know a little about your Apple ID. The Apple ID is basically your account for all Apple services such as iMessage, iCloud, FaceTime, and the App & iTunes Stores. These services can be synced across multiple devices using your Apple ID account. For example, if you are using your Apple ID for iMessage on both your iPhone and iPad, you can send and receive iMessages from both devices. Additionally, iMessages sent and received on one device will appear on the other device.

Sharing an Apple ID

Many parents try sharing an Apple ID with their child as a means to receive their child's iMessages. While this may work, it does have some drawbacks. For instance, if iMessage is not setup correctly on all the devices, the child will receive the parent's iMessages just as the parent will receive the child's iMessages. Remember, the Apple ID is an account for the iMessage service. Sharing an Apple ID means you are sharing the same account and all iMessages can be delivered to all devices using that account.

It is generally not recommended for individuals to share the same Apple ID for iMessages. However, in some circumstances, it does make sense. Therefore, in an upcoming chapter, I will explain how to configure iMessage for the parent to receive the child's iMessages without the child receiving the parent's iMessages. While this isn't the optimal approach, it still deserves to be covered.

Separate Apple IDs

The standard practice is for individuals to have their own independent Apple IDs. In most cases, even family members should have separate Apple IDs. This allows one family member with multiple devices to easily sync information across all their devices without information inadvertently being delivered to another family member's device.

But if separate Apple IDs don't allow information to be delivered to another person, how can a parent monitor a child's messages? The answer is quite simple. The parent can setup an iPad, iPod touch, Mac computer, or an old deactivated iPhone as a dedicated monitoring device using the child's Apple ID instead of the parent's Apple ID.

A dedicated monitoring device allows the parent and child to continue using their existing devices as they normally would. No special configuration is required on either device. The parent just signs in to the child's iMessage account on the monitoring device using the child's Apple ID. The child's iMessages will be delivered to the monitoring device and because the parent is using a separate Apple ID, there is no danger of the parent's iMessages being delivered to the child's device.

If a parent does not have an iPhone, a dedicated monitoring device can still be used to receive a child's iMessages.

A Word About Passwords

If you have young children or you are getting your child his/her first iPhone, I recommend you setup the device and create the Apple ID yourself. This way you will know the Apple ID password. Do not give the password to your child. Whenever they want to download an app or music, they will need to come to you to enter the password. This allows you to control what apps are installed on their device, how much money they spend in the App Store, and allows you access to their Apple ID to monitor iMessages.

Should You Tell Your Child You Are Monitoring Their Texts?

You should consider informing your child you are monitoring their messages. You can tell them it's for their own protection, but it also lets the child know they are not free to do what they want with the iPhone.

It is understandable there may be situations where you may not want to inform your child that you are monitoring them. You must realize if your child discovers you are monitoring him/her without his/her knowledge it will significantly impact the trust of your relationship. You will need to decide what is appropriate for your situation.

In the next chapter, we will discuss the process to setup a dedicated monitoring device and provide some tips to keep your child from knowing their iMessages are being monitored, if you elect not to inform your child.

3 Setup Monitoring When Using Separate Apple IDs

Monitoring your child's iMessages when they have their own Apple ID is a fairly simple process. You basically just need to sign in to your child's iMessage account on a dedicated monitoring device. This monitoring device can be an iPad, iPod touch, Mac computer, or a deactivated iPhone. The monitoring device will be setup specifically to receive your child's iMessages and you will not be able to use it for your iMessages.

You will need to know your child's Apple ID and password to sign in to his/her iMessage account. Additionally, the device you use to monitor your child's messages will need to be connected to the Internet at all times, either with a Wi-Fi network or a cellular data network.

Before getting started, it is recommended to have both your monitoring device and your child's iPhone (and other Apple devices) in your possession. When you sign in with your child's Apple ID on the monitoring device, Apple will send a notification alert to your child's devices informing them a new device has signed in to their account. Additionally, an email will be sent to the email address associated with the Apple ID informing them a new device is using their account. If you don't want your child to know you are monitoring their iMessages, you will want to clear the notification and delete the email on each of their devices.

Step 1 – Check the iMessage Setup on Your Child's Device

Open the Settings app and select Messages.

The iMessage slider should be set to the on position.

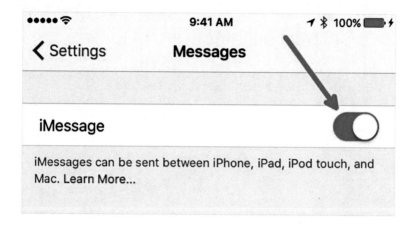

Next, select Send & Receive.

Send & Receive	2 Addresses >

Your child's Apple ID should be visible at the top of the window. This indicates iMessage is setup correctly on your child's device.

If your child's Apple ID is not visible, you will need to sign in using your child's Apple ID and password.

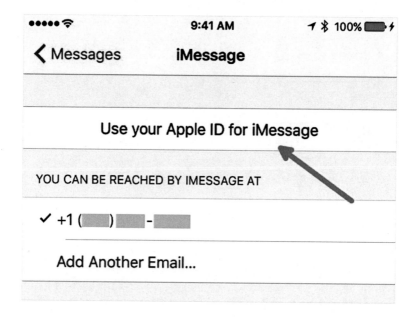

Step 2 – Sign in to Your Child's iMessage Account on the Monitoring Device

On your monitoring device, open the Settings app and select Messages.

Set the iMessage slider to the on position.

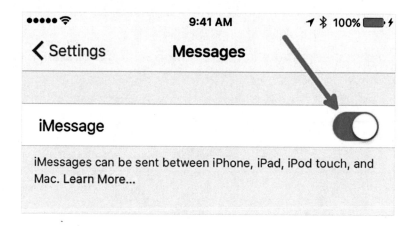

Then select Send & Receive.

Send & Receive   2 Addresses >

Tap "Use Your Apple ID for iMessage" and enter your child's Apple ID and password.

If an Apple ID is already present on the device, tap the Apple ID and select Sign Out from the menu. You can then sign in with your child's Apple ID.

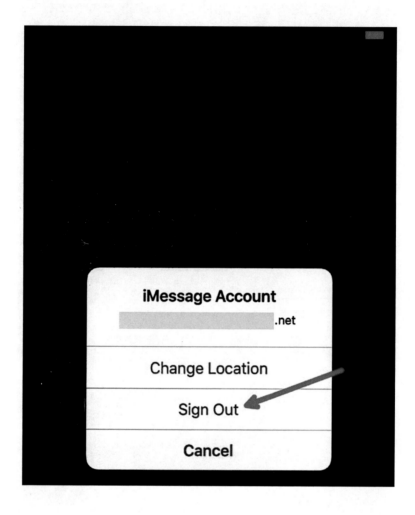

After entering your child's Apple ID and password, iMessage will go through the activation process. You'll be able to start receiving your child's iMessage when the activation process is complete.

A Note About Using an Old iPhone as a Monitoring Device
When trying to use a deactivated iPhone (no cellular service at all) to receive iMessages, you may have trouble completing the activation process on the old iPhone. It may show "Waiting for activation" in the iMessage settings.

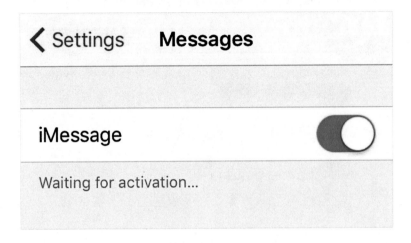

I was able to get a deactivated iPhone connected to iMessage even though it still said "Waiting for activation." You will know when it connects because the Apple ID will appear under the Send & Receive section in the iMessage settings.

If your old iPhone will not connect to iMessage, there are several things you can try.

1. Reset Network Settings

Try resetting the network settings by opening the Settings app, selecting General, then scroll to the bottom and select Reset.

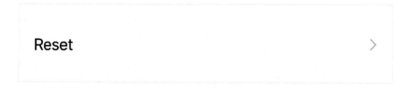

When the reset screen opens, select Reset Network Settings. This will cause the iPhone to restart.

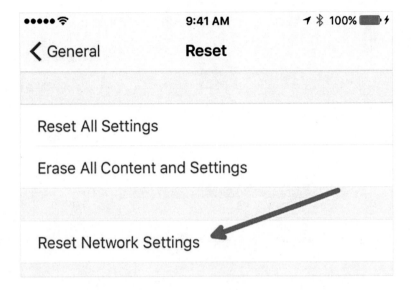

After the iPhone restarts, re-enter the Wi-Fi password to rejoin your wireless network. Once the iPhone is reconnected to Wi-Fi, try activating iMessage. If it doesn't connect to iMessage, try resetting iMessage as described below.

2. Reset iMessage

To reset iMessage on your device, Go to Settings -> Messages -> Send & Receive and uncheck the email addresses in the "You Can Be Reached By iMessage At" section.

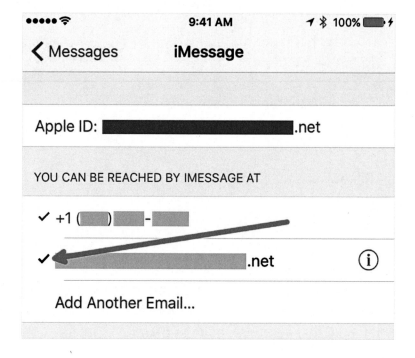

Then, tap your Apple ID at the top of the screen and select Sign Out.

After signing out, make sure the slider for iMessage is set to the off position.

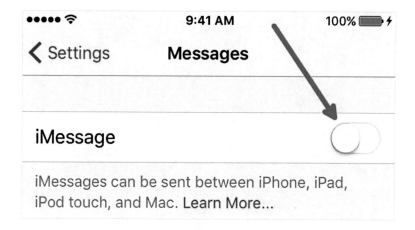

Next, reset your device by pressing and holding both the Sleep/Wake button and the Home button for about 10 seconds. While you are holding the buttons, the screen will go blank. Continue holding the buttons until you see the Apple logo. You can release the buttons after you see the Apple logo appear on the screen.

Sleep/Wake Button

Home Button

Once the device restarts, wait 5 - 10 minutes, then turn the iMessage slider back on and sign in with your child's Apple ID (or your shared Apple ID). The iMessage activation should proceed normally. Once iMessage is activated, go back to Settings -> Messages -> Send & Receive and make sure everything is setup correctly for receiving your child's iMessages.

3. Backup and Restore

If you still can't get the iPhone connected to iMessage, try backing up and restoring the iPhone. These articles from the Apple website explain how to backup and restore your device.
http://support.apple.com/en-us/HT203977
https://support.apple.com/en-us/HT204184

Once you have restored the old iPhone, you may still need to reset iMessage as described in item 2 above.

Some deactivated iPhones have trouble reconnecting to iMessage after they have been deactivated. During the iMessage activation process for an iPhone, an SMS text message is sent to Apple. Since a deactivated iPhone cannot send an SMS text message (no active cellular service), it is supposed to activate over Wi-Fi like an iPad or an iPod touch. Some old iPhones appear to continue trying to activate by sending the SMS text. This may be causing the activation failure. This is only my guess as to what's happening.

Important

Keep trying to activate the old iPhone. It may always display "Waiting for activation", but it should still connect and recognize the Apple ID under Send & Receive.

Step 3 – Clear the Notification on Your Child's Device

When you sign in with your child's Apple ID on the monitoring device, Apple will send a notification alert to all your child's devices informing them a new device has signed in to their account. The notification will appear as a popup window on your child's device. If you don't want your child to know you are monitoring their iMessages, tap the OK button to dismiss the notification.

Your Apple ID and phone number are now being used for iMessage on a new iPhone.

If you recently signed into "Ted's iPhone 6" you can ignore this notification.

OK

Additionally, Apple will send an email to your child's email address informing them a new device is using their account. If you don't want your child to know you are monitoring their iMessages, you will want to open the Mail app on their device and delete the email.

Step 4 – Keep the Monitoring Device Connected to the Internet

All your child's iMessages will now be delivered to the monitoring device as well as the child's device. Any iMessages previously received by your child will not be available, but it will display all future iMessages. Once an iMessage has been delivered to the monitoring device, it will remain on the device even if your child deletes the iMessage from their device.

To avoid missing any iMessages, keep the monitoring device powered on all the time and connected to the Internet using either a Wi-Fi network or a cellular data network connection. If the monitoring device is disconnected from the Internet, it will not receive iMessages. When the device reconnects to the Internet, you will see the iMessages that remain in your child's iMessage account. However, if your child deletes any iMessages while the monitoring device is turned off or disconnected from the Internet, those deleted iMessages will not be available when the monitoring device is reconnected to the Internet.

Important Tips for Monitoring iMessages

1. When your child receives a new message, both your monitoring device and your child's device will receive a notification alert. If you are with your child, you may want to mute your monitoring device or turn off alerts for new messages. Otherwise your child may get suspicious that your device gives an alert every time they receive a message.

2. When new messages are available, the Messages app icon will have a red circle on the top right corner of the app. The red circle is a new message indicator. The number inside the red circle indicates the number of new unread messages.

3. When you open the Messages app, you should see a list of all the different conversation threads from different people. The new messages will have a blue dot to the left of the conversation threads that contains the new messages. When a new message has been opened and read, the blue dot is removed from the conversation thread.

4. **Do not open the new messages** if there is blue dot next to the conversation thread. Opening a new message will remove the blue dot from your child's device indicating the message has been read. Your child will notice this and could realize their messages are being read.

5. When finished viewing the messages, always return to the main window showing the conversation threads and close the Messages app by pressing the Home button. The Home button is the big round button at the bottom center of the screen. If you leave the Messages app open, new messages could open on the monitoring device and appear as if they have already been read on your child's iPhone. As long as you don't keep the Messages app open, your child's messages will not be marked as read.

Remembering to navigate the main window showing the conversation threads before closing the Messages app will allow you to open the app without inadvertently opening a new message.

6. When your child reads the new messages on their iPhone, the blue dot will disappear from the conversation thread on the monitoring device. This is how you will know the messages have been read. If there is no blue dot next to a conversation thread, there are no unread messages and you can freely read the messages.

4 Setup Monitoring When Sharing an Apple ID

If you share an Apple ID with your child, you may already be sharing more than you realize with your child. As we previously discussed, the Apple ID is basically your account for all Apple services. Using the same Apple ID for Messages will allow iMessages to be shared between your devices. Using the same Apple ID for iCloud will allow you to share things like Contacts, Calendars, Notes, Reminders, Photo Stream, and Safari bookmarks and history. Additionally, you will be sharing the same 5GB of free iCloud storage provided by Apple. Sharing the storage will cause your devices to backup to the same iCloud account and potentially use all the iCloud storage. Your devices cannot backup to iCloud if the iCloud storage is full.

While it may seem convenient to share iMessages by sharing an Apple ID, it is generally not recommended to share an Apple ID. However, in some situations it still makes sense. It just takes some careful planning to make sure only the information you want to share appears on each device. For the purpose of this guide, we will only discuss setting up iMessage with a shared Apple ID. Setting up other Apple services such as iCloud and FaceTime with a shared Apple ID is a different discussion.

Step 1 – Check the iMessage Setup on Both Your Child's Device and Your Device

The following procedure should be performed on both your child's device and your device.

Open the Settings app and select Messages.

The iMessage slider should be set to the on position.

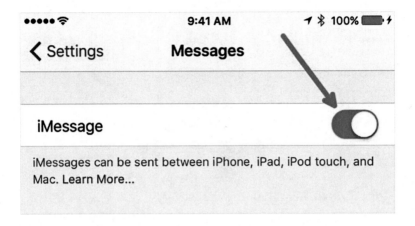

Next, select Send & Receive.

Your Apple ID should be visible at the top of the window. This indicates iMessage is setup correctly on the device.

If your Apple ID is not visible, you will need to sign in using your Apple ID and password.

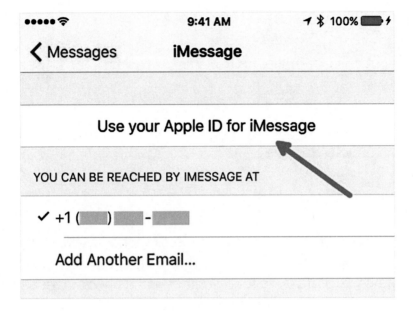

Step 2 – Setup Child's iPhone to Only Receive Their iMessages (And Not Yours)

On your child's iPhone, go to Settings -> Messages -> Send & Receive.

Under the section titled "You Can Be Reached By iMessage At", make sure only your child's phone number has a check mark beside it. If your phone number has a check mark beside it, tap it to deselect your phone number.

You do not want your phone number to be selected or your iMessages will be delivered to your child's iPhone.

One of the dangers of sharing an Apple ID for iMessage is your child can come to this menu at any time and select your phone number to start receiving your iMessages.

Next, scroll down to the section titled "Start New Conversations From" and make sure your child's phone number is checked. This will allow messages sent from your child's iPhone to be sent from their phone number.

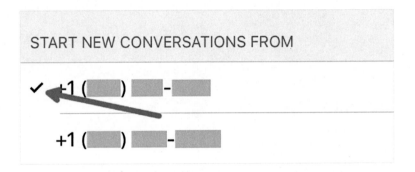

Step 3 – Setup iMessage on Your Device

On your iPhone, go to Settings -> Messages -> Send & Receive. Under the section titled "You Can Be Reached By iMessage At", make sure both your phone number and your child's phone number have a check mark beside them. This will allow messages for both numbers to be delivered to your iPhone.

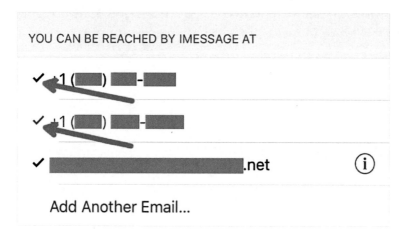

Next, scroll down to the section titled "Start New Conversations From" and make sure your phone number is checked. This will allow messages sent from your iPhone to be sent from your phone number.

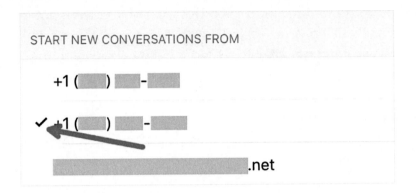

Step 4 – Clear the Notification on Your Child's Device

This step may not be necessary if you were already signed in to iMessage with the Apple ID. However, if you were not previously using your Apple ID with iMessage on your device, Apple will send a notification alert to all devices using the Apple ID informing them a new device has signed in to the account. The notification will appear as a popup window on your child's device. If you don't want your child to know you are monitoring their iMessages, tap the OK button to dismiss the notification.

Your Apple ID and phone number are now being used for iMessage on a new iPhone.

If you recently signed into "Ted's iPhone 6" you can ignore this notification.

OK

Additionally, Apple will send an email to the primary email address for the Apple ID to indicate a new device is using their account. If your child has access to that email, you will want to open the Mail app on their device and delete the email.

Step 5 – Keep the Monitoring Device Connected to the Internet

All your child's iMessages will now be delivered to your device as well as your child's device. Any iMessages previously received by your child will not be available, but it will display all future iMessages. Once an iMessage has been delivered to your device, it will remain on your device even if your child deletes the iMessage from their device.

To avoid missing any iMessages, keep your device powered on all the time and connected to the Internet using either a Wi-Fi network or cellular data network connection. If your device is disconnected from the Internet, it will not receive iMessages. When it reconnects to the Internet, you will see the iMessages that remain in the iMessage account. However, if your child deletes any iMessages while your device is turned off or disconnected from the Internet, those deleted iMessages will not be available when your device is reconnected to the Internet.

Important Tips for Monitoring iMessages

1. When your child receives a new message, both your device and your child's device will receive a notification alert. If you are with your child, you may want to mute your device or turn off alerts for new messages. Otherwise your child may get suspicious that your device gives an alert every time they receive a message.

2. When new messages are available, the Messages app icon will have a red circle on the top right corner of the app. The red circle is a new message indicator. The number inside the red circle indicates the number of new unread messages.

3. When you open the Messages app, you should see a list of all the different conversation threads from different people. The new messages will have a blue dot to the left of the conversation threads that contains the new messages. When a new message has been opened and read, the blue dot is removed from the conversation thread.

4. **Do not open your child's new messages** if there is blue dot next to the conversation thread. Opening a new message will remove the blue dot from your child's device indicating the message has been read. Your child will notice this and could realize their messages are being read.

5. When finished viewing your child's messages, always return to the main window showing the conversation threads or switch to one of your message conversations before closing the Messages app. This will allow you to re-open the Messages app without inadvertently reading a new message sent to your child.

6. When your child reads the new messages on their iPhone, the blue dot will disappear from the conversation thread on

your device. This is how you will know the messages have been read. If there is no blue dot next to a conversation thread, there are no unread messages and you can freely read your child's messages.

5   How to Receive Your Child's SMS Text Messages

Beginning with iOS 8.1, Apple introduced the Text Message Forwarding feature. This allows the iPhone to forward SMS text messages to other devices using the same Apple ID. Therefore, your child's SMS text messages can be forwarded from their iPhone to your device.

Setup Text Message Forwarding

For text message forwarding to work, both your device and your child's iPhone need to be running at least iOS 8.1 and both devices need to be connected to the Internet. Additionally, you will need access to your child's iPhone to setup Text Message Forwarding.

Step 1 – Open the Settings App on Your Child's iPhone

On your child's iPhone, go to Settings -> Messages -> Text Message Forwarding. This option will only appear when a compatible iOS device or Mac computer is connected to the same Wi-Fi network and using the same Apple ID.

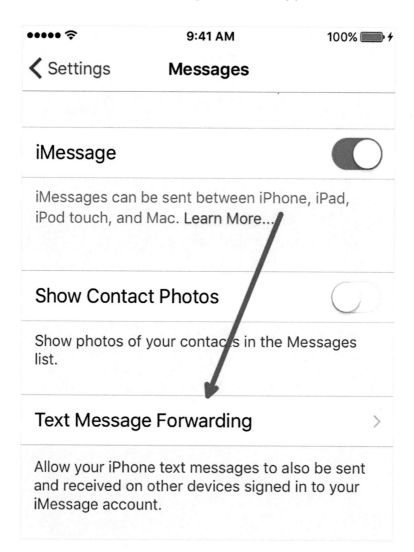

Step 2 – Select Your Device

Your device should be listed in the Text Message Forwarding setup window. Set the slider to the on position to enable Text Message Forwarding to your device.

Step 3 – Authorization Window Appears

An authorization window should appear on your child's iPhone asking for a code.

Step 4 – Get Authorization Code

The authorization code is available in a window that will appear on your device.

Step 5 – Enter Authorization Code on Your Child's iPhone

Enter the authorization code from your device into the authorization window on your child's iPhone.

When the code is entered, this authorizes text messages to be forwarded to your device. You will now be able to receive your child's SMS text messages on your device.

A Word of Caution

If your child is somewhat tech-savvy, it is possible for them to open the Text Message Forwarding menu on their iPhone and see your device is setup to receive their SMS text messages. They can stop the forwarding simply by setting the slider for your device to the off position.

What if the Authorization Code did not Appear?

If you are setting up Text Message Forwarding and the authorization code is not appearing on your device, make sure both your child's iPhone and your device are connected to the same Wi-Fi network. Additionally, make sure both devices are using the same Apple ID in the Messages settings.

If you still can't get the authorization code to appear, you may need to reset iMessage on your device.

Reset iMessage
To reset iMessage, Go to Settings -> Messages -> Send & Receive and uncheck the email addresses in the "You Can Be Reached By iMessage At" section.

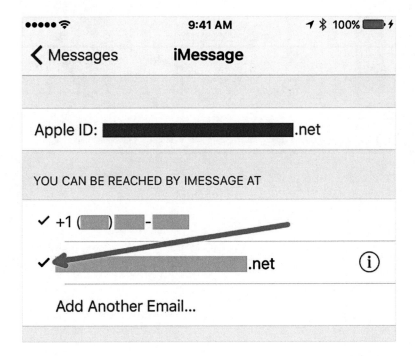

Then, tap your Apple ID at the top of the screen and select Sign Out.

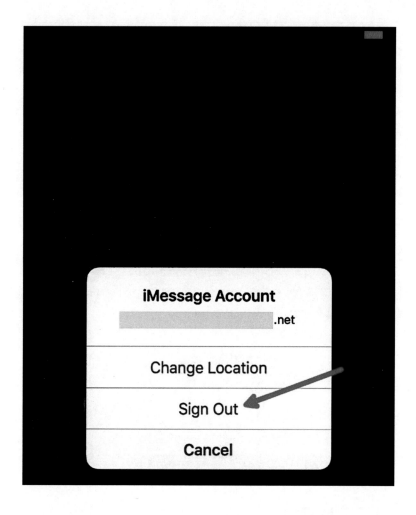

After signing out, make sure the slider for iMessage is set to the off position.

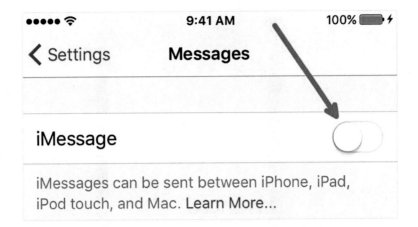

Next, reset your device by pressing and holding both the Sleep/Wake button and the Home button for about 10 seconds. While you are holding the buttons, the screen will go blank. Continue holding the buttons until you see the Apple logo. You can release the buttons after you see the Apple logo appear on the screen.

Sleep/Wake Button

Home Button

Once the device restarts, wait 5 - 10 minutes, then turn the iMessage slider back on and sign in with your child's Apple ID (or your shared Apple ID). The iMessage activation should proceed normally. Once iMessage is activated, go back to Settings -> Messages -> Send & Receive and make sure everything is setup correctly for receiving your child's iMessages. You can then try setting up Text Message Forwarding again.

Additional Thoughts on SMS Text Messages

It is also possible to do some monitoring of SMS text activity using tools available from your cellular provider. The types of tools available will vary from one cellular provider to another.

Messaging Apps From Your Cellular Provider

Many cellular providers offer a messaging app that allows you to receive messages on a smartphone, tablet, or computer. You can setup the app to receive your child's messages. Apps are generally available for iOS devices, Mac computers, Windows computers, and android devices. If your cellular provider has an app for Apple devices, the app will not receive iMessages. You may even need to turn iMessage off on your child's device.

You will need to contact your cellular provider for more information about their specific messaging app.

Using Your Cellular Provider's Website

If your cellular provider does not offer a messaging app, you may find the phone numbers your child is texting by signing in to your account on your cellular provider's website. When viewing your account, there should be a list of all the phone numbers for which your child has sent or received text messages. The actual content of the text message may not be available online, so you may not be able to read the message.

6 Monitor Other Types of Messages

In addition to using the Messages app on the iPhone, there are a wide variety of Internet-based messaging apps available on the App Store. These apps allow your child to send messages over the Internet and are difficult for a parent to monitor. It is important to understand a teenager is likely using more than one of these apps. Some examples of these apps include:

- Facebook Messenger
- Snapchat
- WhatsApp
- Instagram
- Hangouts
- Kik
- ooVoo
- Viber
- and many more.

It is extremely difficult to keep track of all the messaging possibilities available. Not even professional monitor services can monitor all the different messaging apps. If you want to consider using a professional monitoring service, you will need to verify what apps each individual monitoring service supports.

When discussing professional monitoring services, there are basically two types of services: those that do not require jailbreaking your child's iPhone, and those that do require jailbreaking the iPhone so a special monitoring app can be installed. In general, the services in which jailbreaking is not required have more limited monitoring capabilities than services that require jailbreaking the iPhone to install a dedicated monitoring app. The downside to installing a dedicated monitoring app is your child will see the app and know they are being monitored.

If you don't know what it means to jailbreak an iPhone, it probably isn't something you will want to attempt. Basically, jailbreaking is the process of removing restrictions and protections in Apple's iOS software to allow the download of software not available through the official Apple App Store. There are articles all over the Internet explaining how to jailbreak an iPhone. Jailbreaking is not recommended by Apple nor by me and you should understand the risks associated with jailbreaking before attempting to jailbreak your device.

In the end, your best solution for monitoring these Internet-based messaging apps may be the old fashioned method of physically taking your child's device and manually checking these apps.

7   Final Words

Thank You So Much!

I can't thank you enough for your continued support of the iAnswerGuy.com website. I appreciate you purchasing this guide and hope you found it helpful. If you would like to provide some feedback, I would like to hear what you think about this guide.

Please visit my website at http://www.ianswerguy.com. You can contact me from the website if you have any questions or comments.

If you haven't already, you can follow me (iAnswerGuy) on Facebook or Twitter.

Thanks again, and I wish you all the best!

Ted Mitchell
www.ianswerguy.com

43283930R00038